Shalandra Dabbs
PO BOX 493
Arlington, Texas
shalandradabbs@gmail.com

THE SELF-HELP GUIDE TO PPP

PURSUIT A LIFE OF

PEACE PURPOSE AND PROSPERITY

by

Shalandra Dabbs

The Self-Help Guide to PPP
Pursuit a Life of
Peace Purpose and Prosperity / 2

Source: Adapted from Pomponio, 2002; Stress in College Students, 2019; Tips for Coping with Crisis, 2015.

Diagram of the General Adaptation Syndrome. Authored by: David G. Myers – Exploring Psychology 7th ed. (Worth) page 398. Located at: https://en.wikipedia.org/wiki/Stress_(biology)#/media/File: General_Adaptation_Syndrome.jpg. License: CC BY: Attribution

Psychology by OpenStax is licensed under a Creative Commons Attribution 4.0 International License, except where otherwise noted.

"The Song of the Songs of Solomon," based upon the Hebrew title of the book Julie Schwab, Discovery Series Author writes "Love is as strong as death, it's jealousy unyielding as the grave."

https://www.amazon.com/Journey-into-Singleness-fulfillment-contentment/dp/1718946791
https://www.amazon.com/Ms-Shalandra-L-Dabbs/e/B07MHB8Q26/ref=aufs_dp_mata_dsk

The Working Man & Woman's Guide to Becoming a Millionaire. By Herron, Al; Middlebrook, Sallie B. ISBN 10: 0977860701

The Self-Help Guide to PPP
Pursuit a Life of
Peace Purpose and Prosperity / 4

The Self-Help Guide to PPP
Pursuit a Life of
Peace Purpose and Prosperity / 5

-

TABLE OF CONTENTS

ACKNOWLEDGEMENTS

Giving All Glory in Honor to my Heavenly Father for Blessing me with a spirit to serve others expressed through the Literary Arts – Writing

Thank you to my Beautiful Family
Mother Mary L. Dabbs
Daughter Lisa Dabbs-Miles
Sharmisa L. Anderson
Dadrian L. Dabbs
SheAndria L. Minger-Coleman
And all my Beautiful 14 Grandchildren

My Prayer is to whomever reads this book that you really live life to the fullest, live and not just exist. The Abundance of life is yours, all you must do is act, keep the faith in God and Believe. Blessings and Favor upon you!
Ms. Shalandra L Dabbs

Other Reads by: *Ms. Shalandra L. Dabbs*

"Journey into Singleness Live a Life of Joy Fulfillment and Contentment"

"365 Days of Empowering Inspirations"

"The ABCs to Self-Love 90-Days of Affirmation to Transformation"

To Be Released in December 2022
– My first fiction Novel entitled "Never Meant to Cause You No Pain"

The purpose of this book is to encourage you to live a life of peace, purpose, and prosperity. To help you plan, prepare, and pursue your dreams, goals, ambitions, and desires in this life. To inspire you to really seek God in everything you do. To motivate you to be your best self and to love yourself, experience all that life has to offer and all that you have to offer in life. To encourage you to be all you strive to be utilizing your talents and gifts as God planned. To live Life and Life more abundantly as Jesus directed. To develop your mindset on the positive aspects of life. To focus your attention on optimism, and to hope for the best through life's journey. To Live your best life on earth as it is in heaven. ***Proverbs 29:18*** Where there is no vision, the people perish

CHAPTER 1

Pursuit a Life of Peace

What is "peace?" When I think of peace, I think of quiet, stillness, serene, purity and light. When one has peace in your life, you are not focused on all the hell that is going on in life and around you. Your mind, body and spirit are at peace. The world's definition of peace is tranquility and quietness, freedom from war or civil disorder and or harmony in human relationships. Biblically, Jesus tells us in *John 16:33*, "These things I have spoken unto you, that in me you might have tribulation but be of good cheer; I have overcome the world." Jesus is saying it does not matter what we go through in life that He did not endure here on earth, but He overcame and for that reason we should be of good cheer (be happy). Jesus conquered not only death but all sin, evil, temptation, wickedness, etcetera at the cross. Therefore, being justified by faith, we have peace with God through our Lord Jesus Christ. *Romans 5:1*

My personal experience trying to live in such away doing things my way, I lacked peace. For example: I could not sleep at night, my life was topsy-turvy in ways where I felt as if I were digressing instead of progressing. To make a long story short, I was out of the will of God. When one is out of the God's will, one will experience sleepless nights, deserted lands, valley experiences and unfavorable circumstances. I know a lady who must take a sleep aide just to get some sleep at night. Notice I did not mention that it would be a good night's sleep that she would experience. When one is in the will of God, God will give you peace. You have peace because God is in control. You can live a life not giving any thought what you shall eat, or what you shall drink; nor yet for your body, what shall you put on because God is leading the way. The bible says in *Philippians 4:19* my God shall supply all your need according to His riches and glory by Christ Jesus. In other words, let GO and let GOD! Peace Be Still

Life is not measured by the number of breaths you take, but by the moments that take your breath away.

Author, Unknown

Understanding Stress

Stress is the interpretation of specific events, called stressors, as threatening, or challenging. The seven major sources of stress are life changes, conflict, hassles, frustration, cataclysmic events, job stressors, and acute/chronic stressors.

1) **Life changes** require adjustment in our behaviors that cause stress. **2) Conflicts** are forced choices between two or more competing goals or impulses. They are often classified as approach–approach, avoidance–avoidance, or approach–avoidance. **3) Hassles** are little everyday life problems that pile up to cause major stress, and burnout. **4) Frustration** refers to blocked goals. **5) Cataclysmic events** are disasters that occur suddenly and affect many people simultaneously. **6) Work-related job stressors** include role conflict and/or role ambiguity. **7) Acute stressors** refer to a short-

term state of arousal in response to a perceived threat or challenge. **Chronic stressors** produce a state of continuous physiological arousal, in which demands are perceived as greater than available coping resources.

Hans Selye's general adaptation syndrome (GAS) describes our body's three-stage reaction to stress: the initial alarm reaction, the resistance phase, and the exhaustion phase (if resistance to stress is not successful). If stress is resolved, our bodies return to normal, baseline functioning, called homeostasis.

The SAM system and the HPA axis control significant physiological responses to stress. The SAM system prepares us for immediate action; the HPA axis responds more slowly but provides a response that lasts longer.

Prolonged stress suppresses the immune system, which increases the risk for many diseases (e.g., colds, colitis, cancer). The new field of psychoneuroimmunology studies the effects of psychological and other factors on the immune system.

During **acute stress**, cortisol can prevent the retrieval of existing memories, as well as the laying down of new memories and general information processing. Under prolonged stress, cortisol can permanently damage the hippocampus, a key part of the brain involved in memory. Our bodies are always under stress, some of which has beneficial effects. Eustress is pleasant, desirable stress, whereas distress is unpleasant, undesirable stress. Stress is also beneficial depending on task complexity, and social support is invaluable for coping with stress.

Stress and Illness

Scientists once believed that stress, or the H. pylori bacterium, acting alone, could cause gastric ulcers. Current psychological research shows that biopsychosocial factors, including stress, interact to increase our vulnerability to the bacterium, which may then lead to gastric ulcers. Cancer appears to result from an interaction of heredity, environmental factors (such as smoking), and immune system deficiencies. Although stress is linked to a weakened immune response, research does not show that it causes cancer, or that a cheerful outlook alone will prevent cancer. Increased stress hormones can cause fat to adhere to blood vessel walls, increasing the risk of cardiovascular disorders, including heart attacks. Statistics shows, the number one killer in the country are heart attacks. And further statistics shows that most heart attacks occur between the hours of 8 to 5 "work hours." Because when one is not pursuing one's goals, one is committing spiritual suicide. Chronic pain is a type of continuous or recurrent pain, experienced over a period of 6 months or longer. To treat chronic pain, health psychologists emphasize psychologically oriented treatments, such as behavior modification, biofeedback, and relaxation. Exposure to extraordinary stress can cause posttraumatic stress disorder (PTSD), a type of trauma- and stressor-related disorder characterized by the persistent re-experiencing of traumatic events, which resulted from war, natural disasters, sexual assault, and so on.

Stress Management

Why do some people survive in the face of great stress (personal tragedies, demanding jobs, or an abusive home life) while others do not? One answer may be that these "survivors" have a unique trait called positive affect, meaning they more often experience and express positive emotions, including feelings of happiness, joy, enthusiasm, and contentment (e.g., Katana et al., 2019). People who are high in positive affect also tend to have lower levels of inflammation, fewer colds and auto accidents, better sleep, and an enhanced quality of life (Brannon et al., 2018; Tavernier et al., 2016). Remember the story about "Cinderella" and" Annie?" Optimism, Hope, Faith, Positivity will take you a long way in life. How can one fail with God on your side? With a cheerful outlook, hoping for the best and remaining optimistic by keeping the faith in God until you reap the fruit of your labor.

Stress management begins with a three-step cognitive appraisal. Step 1 is primary appraisal (deciding if

a situation is harmless or potentially harmful), and Step 2 is
secondary appraisal (assessing our resources and choosing
a coping method). In Step 3, we tend to choose either
emotion-focused coping (managing emotional reactions to
a stressor) or problem-focused coping (dealing directly
with the stressor to decrease or eliminate it).

Sigmund Freud (1856–1939) is the most
controversial and misunderstood psychological theorist.
When reading Freud's theories, it is important to remember
that he was a medical doctor, not a psychologist. There was
no such thing as a degree in psychology at the time that he
received his education, which can help us understand some
of the controversy over his theories today. However, Freud
was the first to systematically study and theorize the
workings of the unconscious mind in the manner that we
associate with modern psychology. Freud proposed that we
commonly cope with stress with defense mechanisms,
which are strategies the ego uses to protect itself from
anxiety, but they often distort reality and may increase self-

deception. Personality and individual differences also affect stress management. Having an internal locus of control (believing that we control our own fate), as opposed to an external locus of control (believing that chance or outside forces beyond our control determine our fate), is an effective personal strategy for stress management. People with a positive affect and optimism tend to live longer and to deal better with stress. Mindfulness-based stress reduction (MBSR) and social support are two important keys to stress management. Freud believed that feelings of anxiety result from the ego's inability to mediate the conflict between the id and superego. When this happens, Freud believed that the ego seeks to restore balance through various protective measures known as defense mechanisms. When certain events, feelings, or yearnings cause an individual anxiety, the individual wishes to reduce that anxiety. To do that, the individual's unconscious mind uses ego defense mechanisms, unconscious protective behaviors that aim to reduce anxiety. The ego, usually conscious, resorts to unconscious strivings to protect the ego from being overwhelmed by anxiety. When we use defense mechanisms, we are unaware that we are using them. Further, they operate in numerous ways that distort reality. According to Freud, we all use ego defense mechanisms.

Six additional resources are:

1) Exercise, exercising and keeping fit help minimize anxiety and depression, relieve muscle tension, improve cardiovascular efficiency, and increase strength, flexibility, and stamina. "Those who do not find time for exercise will have to find time for illness." —Edward Smith-Stanley

2) Social skills, people who acquire social skills (such as knowing appropriate behaviors for certain situations, having conversation starters up their sleeves, and expressing themselves well) suffer less anxiety than people who do not. Social skills not only help us interact with others but also communicate our needs and desires, enlist help when we need it, and decrease hostility in tense situations.

3) Behavior change, when under stress, do you smoke, drink, overeat, zone out in front of the TV or computer, sleep too much, procrastinate, or take your stress out on others? If so, you can substitute these activities with healthier choices, such as listening to your favorite podcast.

4) Stressor control, remember stress is a part of life and cannot be eliminated, but you can recognize and avoid unnecessary stress by analyzing your schedule and removing non-essential tasks, avoiding people and topics that increase your stress, finding a less stressful job, and/or giving yourself permission to say "no" to extra tasks and responsibilities.

5) Material resources, money increases the number of options available for eliminating sources of stress or reducing the effects of stress. When faced with the minor hassles of everyday living, acute or chronic stressors, or major catastrophes, people with more money, and the skills to effectively use it, fare better. They experience less overall stress and can "buy" more resources to help them cope with what stressors they do have.

6) Relaxation, there are a variety of relaxation techniques. Biofeedback is often used in the treatment of chronic pain, but it is also useful in teaching people to relax and manage their stress. Progressive relaxation helps reduce or relieve the muscular tension commonly associated with stress.

Seven Important Tips for Coping with Crisis:

1) If you have experienced a traumatic event, recognize your feelings about the situation, and talk to others about your fears. Know that these feelings are a normal response to an abnormal situation. **2)**If you know someone who has been traumatized, be willing to patiently listen to their account of the event, pay attention to their feelings, and encourage them to seek counseling, if necessary. **3)** Be patient and kind to yourself and others. It is natural to feel anxious, helpless, and frustrated, but give yourself a break. Also, tempers are short in times of crisis, and others may be feeling as much stress as you. **4)** Recognize normal crisis reactions, such as sleep disturbances and nightmares, withdrawal, reversion to childhood behaviors, and trouble focusing on work or school. **5)** Be mindful of your time. Feel free to say "NO"

to others. Limit your news watching—except when it is
necessary to do so, as in a national emergency. Take time
with your children, spouse, life partner, friends, and co-
workers to do something you enjoy. **6)** Get plenty of sleep
and avoid alcohol and other drugs. We all need a good
night's sleep, especially during times of crisis. Alcohol and
other drugs interfere with sleep and good decision making.
7) Study and adopt stress management skills, such as the
ones discussed in this chapter.

Remember Health psychology is a branch of psychology
that studies how biological, psychological, and social
factors influence health, illness, and health-related
behaviors. Health psychologists focus on how changes in
behavior can improve health outcomes. They often work as
independent clinicians, or as consultants to other health
practitioners, to educate the public about illness prevention
and health maintenance. Health psychologists also study
job stress and how to reduce it. If you or someone you

know are struggling with anxiety due to stress, contact a

licensed Health Psychologist in your area.

Managing Depression

Humor is one of the best methods you can use to reduce stress. The ability to laugh at oneself and at life's inevitable difficulties allows us to relax and gain a broader perspective. In addition, "laughter therapy" has been linked to a significant reduction in heart rate and systolic blood pressure (e.g., Yoshikawa et al., 2018). Whoever produced the acronym LOL is a genius in my opinion because the expression reminds me to not only laugh but LAUGH OUT LOUD!

Another devoured spirit that often goes along with addiction and substance abuse is depression. Depression is an unwanted and prolonged condition of emotional dejection per the Webster's dictionary. The NAACP slogan is "a mind is terrible thing to waste." As stated, before our mind is the vital element that encompasses our entire body. We are who we think we are. One must conjure up in one's mind who one claims to be. Our thought process is either negative or positive however who we claim to be or not to be all starts within the mind.

Depression is another culprit that some are battling within their minds. When one suffers from depression you know that the negative emotions associated with the condition affect every aspect of your life. Depression is a mental health condition that affects the way a person functions thinks, sleeps, eats and feels about oneself. Depression is an illness that takes control of a person's thoughts emotions, feelings, and moods. It will affect a person's health and behavior and impact on their ability to function and lead a happy, healthy, and productive life. There are several types of depression: Clinical, reactive, endogenous, manic (bipolar) season affective disorder, and post-natal per The Depression Alliance.

Clinical depression is a general term used to describe a range of depression conditions.

Reactive depression is triggered by a traumatic, difficult, or stressful event and people affected will feel low, anxious, irritable, and even angry.

Endogenous depression will experience physical symptoms such as weight change, tiredness, sleeping problems and low mood, as well as poor concentration and low self-esteem.

Manic depression for the term commonly used now is bipolar depression. People with manic (bipolar depression experience mood swings, with highs of excessive energy and elation, to lows of despair and lethargy. Delusions and hallucinations can also occur.

Seasonal Affective Disorder (SAD) This type of depression coincides with the approach of winter. It is often linked to shortening of daylight hours and lack of sunlight. Symptoms will include wanting to sleep excessively and cravings for carbohydrates or sweet food. Special light boxes can be used to treat this kind of depression.

Post Natal depression affects many new mothers that will experience post-partum baby blues; mood swings, crying spell and feelings of loneliness, three or four days after giving birth. Post-natal depression will last for much longer and will include symptoms such as panic attack, sleeping difficulties, having over whelming fears about dying, and feeling of inadequacy and being unable to cope. Post-natal depression is a common condition affecting between 10% and 20% of new mothers.

Depression statistics: Major depressive disorder affects approximately 14.8 million American adults, or about 6.7 percent of the U.S. population age 18 and older each year (archives of General Psychiatry, 2005 June; 62 (6); 617-27). As many as 1 in 33 children and 1 in 8 adolescents have clinical depression (Center for Mental Health Services, U.S. of Dept. of Health and Human Services, 1996). People with depression are four times as likely to develop a heart attack versus those without a history of the illness (National Institute of Mental Health, 1998).

My point is this: Depression often co-occurs with other illnesses and medical conditions. For example: eating disorders: 50-75% of eating disorder patients experience depression per The National Institute of Mental Health, 1999. Substance abuse: 27% of individuals with substance abuse disorders (alcohol and drugs) experience depression per The National Institute of Mental Health, 1999. Diabetes: 8.5-27% of person with diabetes experience depression, (Rosen and Amador, 1996). Women experience depression at twice the rate of men. This 2:1 ratio exists regardless of racial or ethnic background or economic status. The lifetime prevalence of a major depression is 20-26% for women and 8-12% for men per the Journal of the American Medical Association, 1996.

Depression and Suicide: Depression is the cause of our two-thirds of the 30,000 reported suicides in the U.S. each year per the White House Conference on Mental

Health, 1999. For every two homicides committed in the
United States, there are three suicides. The death rate from
suicide is 11.3 per 100,000 populations. I had a cousin
named Eric D. Coleman who committed suicide. Eric hung
himself before his 28th birthday. When Eric was living,
now that some of the family tells all, there were signs that
everyone overlooked just thinking that he was acting
strange. Some of the signs where he stopped enjoying life.
He quit his job unexpectedly. He picked arguments with his
older brother each time they encountered one another. It
was as if he had a death wish. He stopped caring about his
appearance. He often gave people he encountered long
hugs and constantly told all of us he loved us. The last
thing anyone would have ever imagined is that he or
anyone else in the family would take their own life. Eric
was my eldest Aunt Jeannie's youngest child. She has not
been the same since his tragic death.

We also had a family friend named Chris who took
his own life while in the company of one of my first

cousins and my brother. I will never forget the phone call I
received at work from my brother that Chris had put a
loaded gun in his mouth and pulled the trigger. My brother
and one of my first cousins found Chris in a nearby on sight
laundry room within the apartments I resided at the time.
Chris often hung out with us on the weekends. This was a
time in my life after the break-up with my daughter Shea
and my son Dadrian's dad I needed to be around family
because I did not want to be alone. I am no stranger to
loneliness. My brother and my cousin's family moved in
with us for an entire summer. Now that I think back, Chris
had a death wish. He carried a gun everywhere we went to
hang out. He picked fights with total strangers. As if he
wanted someone to kill him, so that he did not have to take
his own life. He slept sometimes for days at a time. He did
not want to eat. All he wanted to do was drink alcohol. We
were so young; none of us noticed the signs. I was only 24
years of age myself. was a sad, sad day when we all had to
prepare to attend his funeral to pay our last respects. Things

were never the same again after Chris died. He was so young, if memory serves me correctly, Chris was only nineteen. He had been going through employment issues, baby mama drama and he was his parent's only child. He kept trying to talk to me as I prepared to go to work one afternoon. I distinctly told him that we would talk when I got back home. The next day, I went to the laundry mat where Chris had taken his life. Oddly enough I found his coveralls in the dryer. I wore those coveralls for the longest trying my best to keep his memory alive the best way I knew how. We all were lost for words for days. One night I even witnessed, my brother picking up the telephone receiver "dreaming" thinking he was talking to Chris. My brother was trying to talk him into to turning around and not going to the laundry mat. Chris told everyone he needed to take a walk to clear his head. His car stayed parked in front of my apartment door for weeks until his parents were strong enough to retrieve it. It was only then we had gotten closure. Shortly afterward we all went our separate ways.

If you have thoughts of suicide, please get help. The suicide prevention hotline is located at the index of the book. Losing Eric hurt our entire family. My middle daughter, Sharmisa has made it her mission to prevention suicide through her play "The Last Chance." Sharmisa is also a certified Suicide Awareness Counselor. Sharmisa takes death hard. She cannot fathom why God did not lead someone to Eric in time. As stated, before there are signs of suicide. Suicide is acknowledged as the silent killer. Unfortunately, the residual effect of suicide impacts the loved ones left behind to live with a lifetime of guilt, hurt, questions, despair, grief, anger, and sadness etcetera, all the negative spirits not of God. While the person that committed the heinous act is with the Lord, leaving behind such great pain and sorrow. To be absent from the body is to be present with the Lord. *2 Corinthians 5:8*

You can't expect to succed if you only put in work on the days you feel like it.

CHAPTER 2

Pursuit a Life in Purpose on Purpose

In these unprecedented times in which we live due to Corona Virus the pandemic spread of COVID-19, our lives shall never be the same. For some of us that are survivors of the pandemic if one is not seeking change, now is the divine opportunity to do so. Everyone has a divine destiny to fulfill in this life. Destiny is your fate; it is the inevitable. God has predestined all of us for greatness. We as believers are set apart; appointed to be used for a special purpose; predetermined unalterably, as by divine decree. Finding who you are in Christ and knowing who you are in Christ is a "crucial" step in fulfilling destiny and knowing your purpose. God establishes our fate. He said in His word in **Romans 8:29** for whom He did foreknow, He also did predestinate to be conformed to the image of His Son, that He might be the first-born among many brethren. *30* Moreover whom He did predestinate, them He also called; and whom He called, them He also justified: and whom He justified, them He also glorified.

As stated before, what we go through is not for us however we are living testimonies. We are testaments of God's power, and that Jesus lives within us. To come to a point in finding, developing, and embracing God's purpose; one must be set free and made whole. God wants to use you as His vessel. **Romans 8:1** say there is therefore now no condemnation to them which are in Christ Jesus, who walk not after the flesh, but after the Spirit. *2* For the law of the Spirit of life in Christ Jesus has made us free from the law of sin and death. Being made free from sin, you became the servants of righteousness. But now being made free from sin, and become servants to God, you have your fruit unto holiness, and the end everlasting life.

Yes, part of our purpose in life is to be utilized by God as servants of Christ. When God gives you purpose, it will require serving others. If one is not fully committed to a life of serving others, your purpose may not be of God.

Martin R De Haan II, author of Discover Series, "How Can
I Find Satisfaction in My Work" suggests, an old Chinese
proverbs state, a man grows must tired while standing
still." "One sense of personal worth is intricately connected
to a feeling that we are accomplishing something
purposeful with our lives. What we feel that should be
fulfilling and satisfying unfortunately does not always give
us that sense of satisfaction. What should be personally
fulfilling is more often a drain on us physically, mentally,
spiritually, and emotionally such as work however when
one accepts God's perspective on work, one will find
fulfillment and that perspective includes a new "job
description" as found in the Bible."

-Martin R De Haan II

Let us start with our job and/or career path that one
may have chosen. It is not simply good enough to have and
maintain a job these days and times, it is even better to
have a career or better launch a business. I know several
people that have had successful careers but have quit their

job just to pursue their true purpose in life. Vice-versa,
some have made their careers their life's passion, mission
and/or purpose. Jesus says, "For God so loved the world
that He gave His only begotten Son, that whosoever
believeth in Him should not perish, but have everlasting
life,"

John 3:16. God commended His love toward us, in that,
while we were yet sinners, Christ died for us. Although our
purpose is not as significant as Jesus's purpose, we still
must seek God to reveal it to us. Some may know as a child
what their purpose in life is and others it takes prayer, time,
and revelation. And when he was twelve years old, they
went up to Jerusalem after the custom of the feast. *Luke
2:43*And when they had fulfilled the days, as they returned,
the child Jesus tarried behind in Jerusalem; and Joseph and
his mother knew not of it. *44* But they, supposing him to
have been in the company, went a day's journey; and they
sought him among their kinsfolk and acquaintance. *45* And
when they found him not, they turned back again to

Jerusalem, seeking him. *46* And it happened, that after three days they found him in the temple, sitting during the doctors, both hearing them, and asking them questions. *47*And all that heard him were astonished at his understanding and answers. *48* And when they saw him, they were amazed: and his mother said unto him, Son, why hast thou thus dealt with us? behold, thy father and I have sought thee sorrowing. *49*And he said unto them, how is it that ye sought me? wist ye not that I must be about my Father's business? My point is: ***Romans 12:11*** Not slothful in business; fervent in spirit; serving the Lord.

One's purpose must be fulfilled before leaving this world. As when Jesus therefore had received the vinegar, He said, it is finished: and He bowed His head and gave up the ghost.

John 19:30. Although Jesus still lives, He conquered death so that we may have eternal life. God can use anyone at any given time as He chooses. Jesus rained the earth for a little over thirty years however He not only fulfilled His purpose but while here on earth, He healed the sick, raised the dead and delivered people from darkness into the marvelous light. Jesus accomplished so much in such a little period. We do not know how much time we have in this life; therefore, we should not waste time. Repent for the kingdom of God is at hand. In **Mark 1:15** Jesus, and saying, the time is fulfilled, and the kingdom of God is at hand: repent ye and believe the gospel. Time is of the essence. Get busy working, ministering, praying, praising, giving, evangelizing, and anything else God has called you to do.

God blesses each of us with talents and gifts to execute for building of His church to build His kingdom on earth. Who is the church? We are the church! **John 10:10** The thief cometh not, but for to steal, and to kill, and to destroy I am come that they might have life, and that they might have it more abundantly. John wrote that Jesus came to fill the empty and to offer life "to the full" (John 10:10). (*a More in-depth view about life of abundance in a later* *chapter).* One must remember the big picture. And the picture is everything that one does and happens is according to God's will. ***James 1:17*** Every good gift and every perfect gift is from above, and cometh down from the Father of lights, with whom is no variableness, neither shadow of turning. Some of us God blesses to be multi-talented which means, there are various visions that He has given some that can be utilized in all aspects of life. I will start with myself, as a child I had this fascination with mixing and matching colors. One of my gifts God has given me is a gift of fashion however it began with my first coloring book. I remember my mom bought me the set of eight Crayola's, then the set of sixteen and twenty-four. Finally, I begged her for a sixty-four pack of colors. She finally agreed and purchased the crayons for me. I remember drawing, coloring, mixing, and matching those colors for days. I had a field day. I also had a passion for dressing up and collecting Barbie Dolls. My mom bought

and kept me abreast of all the latest Barbie Dolls. I still
have a fetish for collecting Barbie Dolls to this very day.

One Christmas, my mom surprised me with a set of
fashion plates with colored pencils. This is when I
discovered my passion for fashion. As a child I spent hours
mixing, matching, and creating assorted designs with the
fashion plates. It is important to remember that we are to be
more like Jesus. However, Jesus at the mere age of twelve
was about His Father's business and knew what His
purpose was. My point is: as parents we have a significant
role in our children's lives. We should be exposing them to
various projects, opportunities and educating them early so
that they may seek out and get to know their purpose
young.

Today, God has blessed me to be a "fashionista." I
am not a designer however I do follow the latest fashion
trends and incorporate in my wardrobe. How God utilizes
the gift He has blessed me with for fashion is I am known
by my fashion sense. People approach me all the time to

inquire about my shoes, my outfit, and lipstick color etcetera. This gives me an opportunity to walk in confidence as an Ambassador of Christ and opportunity to minister through conversation. I also donate clothes to local charities annually. Part of one of my fundraisers is a fashion show of old clothes that our team updates for a silent auction. God has blessed with me multiple talents and gifts; fashion is just one of them. However, it took years of work for me to discover the gift within. That is why we should start early with our children. If your gift is of God, it will come naturally. Your gift is something that God embedded in you when He created you. ***Jeremiah 1:5*** Before I formed thee in the belly, I knew thee; and before thou camest forth out of the womb I sanctified thee, and I ordained thee a prophet unto the nations.

There is so much work to do and so little time. Remember everything we do and say, we must give in account on judgment day. "Unless you can make connection between what you do all day and what you think God wants you to be doing, you will never find ultimate meaning in your work or your relationship with God." (Doug Sherman & William Hendricks) I would like to add; your purpose cannot be fulfilled if there is not any "heart" meaning found. You find meaning through working and your purpose is found with a relationship with God. God gives and reveals your purpose to you. Your beginning, tomorrow, later and ending has already been written, God is just waiting on some to catch up.

GOD HAS A PURPOSE FOR YOUR PAIN, A REASON FOR YOUR STRUGGLES AND A REWARD FOR YOUR FAITHFULNESS DON'T GIVE UP!

Purpose in Work

What is work? "Work is a consequence of creation, not the fall; the fall has aggravated the problems without destroying its joys." (John R.W. Scott), Author We all know that work is essential to our livelihood. *2 Thessalonians 3:10* for even when we were with you, this we commanded you, that if any would not work neither should he eat. There is a difference in God's work, being about His business and the work that one labor to make a living however in everything we do; we do it for the Glory of God. God is who we answer to, submit to and for whom we work. Whatever you do, do it heartily, as to the Lord and not to men. *Colossians 3:23* Whatsoever thy hand find to do, do it with thy might; for there is not work, nor device, nor knowledge, nor wisdom, in the grave, where thou go. And whatsoever you do in word or deed, do all in the name of the Lord Jesus, giving thanks to God and the Father by Him. It does not matter what we do for a living if we keep our priorities intact. God does supply all our needs according to His riches and glory. "The goal of work is not to gain wealth and possessions, but to serve the common good and bring glory to God," Richard Foster, Author. This means that we work to survive and while we are on the job working, whoever we work for, wherever we go and whatever we do, bring glory to God. God cares about our choice of career and how well we represent Him on the job.

As stated previously, one must learn how to manage our time and keep our priorities intact. One does not work to gain all the material possessions that one desires, one works to maintain a living. *Mark 8:36 Jesus said, "For what is a man profited, if he shall gain the entire world, and lose his own soul?" "Or what shall a man give in exchange for his soul?"* God does not want you to be a workaholic, spending your time here working to please self. There is a balance in working and being about our father's business. It is simple, if God has called or predestined you to do something, do it. If you are so busy and consumed

with working not being mindful to spend time with Him,
how will you hear from God?

Some of us due to the pandemic was on lock down
for eighteen months. Some lost their jobs, other careers and
even experienced losing a loved one to COVID-19. The
economy experienced a recession like we have never
experienced. Not to mention all the natural disasters that
has engulfed our presence as never seen before. As stated,
prior, some of our lives has been altered indefinitely. There
is no time like the present to pick up and start completely
over. As Finding the right work may be a challenge
however working the right way, God's way is the
purposeful alternative. There are so many people
implementing non-profit organizations, working in ministry
full-time, utilizing their spiritual talents and gifts for God's
people. That is great however there are God's people that
are called to do "remarkable" and "extraordinary" things
utilizing their talents and gifts in their work. For example:
Inventors, news reporters, doctors, lawyers, nurses,

teachers, technicians, firefighters, police officers' etcetera.
During the pandemic, the healthcare professionals and
Firefighters are presently known as "front-line heroes." It
takes a very compassionate, caring, and considerate person
to walk in those shoes. Oh my gosh, let us not forget to
mention the news reporters, traveling from state to state,
country to country reporting the devastation of tornados,
hurricanes, wildfires, and COVID-19 numbers. And some
teachers lost their lives due to COVID-19 trying to do their
job to the best of their ability. I mentioned all the various
careers that have been life changing because one must have
a passion, calling and strength to help others. Some of those
Healthcare Professionals along with teachers could have
never imagined such an atrocity such as the pandemic
while serving in their careers. Remember serving others is a
gift.

My grandson Melvin at the mere age of five
informed us he wants to be a Meteorologist when grows up.
He is now fourteen years old; his vision has not changed.

For some reason, he is fascinated with the weather. But Melvin is a GREAT football player. He is also talented and gifted in STEM. It is the Jesus within Him, guiding, leading, and directing him. My grand-daughter Kaydance loves to flip, jump, and dance. I already see a world's famous gymnast/Olympian however she drives her mother crazy with all that energy. Kaydance does not have any fear because what she does is a God given talent. I find it ironic that "dance" is a part of her name. Is it by chance? I do not think so.

Dr. Myles Monroe says "You cannot fulfill your purpose without work. Trying to get money by winning the lottery bypasses personal fulfillment. Neither can you achieve God's intent for your life by reaping the benefits of someone else's efforts. Those who win the lottery often testify that they are unhappy after they receive all that money than before, why, because they lose their reason for getting up in the morning."

Monroe also states, "Without purpose, life becomes meaningless. Life on "easy street" is not easy because satisfaction requires effort. In fact, winning a million dollars could very well kill you if you stopped working. Oh, your body might live for a while, but your potential the real you would die from lack of use. The joy of life would be gone."

He goes on to say that "God gives you work to meet your need for personal fulfillment. When you try to get something for nothing you miss the opportunity to find gratification, because effort is the key to satisfaction. Life bears this out in many ways. Benefits without work short-circuit fulfillment because you usually have more appreciation for something you worked hard to get. You remember all you went through to obtain it, and from your remembering flows the impetus to treasure and care for the products of your labor. Handouts meet your desire for material possessions, but they deny you the pride of gaining through effort. This is the weakness of a welfare system

that robs the individual of the person responsibility,
gratification and pride that comes from self-development
and self-deployment."

I have an aunt that has worked tirelessly her entire
life. She says, "She works in the way she does, to leave her
children well off." She does not want her children to want
for anything. Her children on the other hand, do not want
her money. They have their own lives, purpose, and vision
to fulfill. My aunt does not understand her children's logic
because she has not grasped the fulfillment in working. My
aunt retired from her job over thirty years, just to start her
own for-profit business. She retired in her late fifties and is
currently seventy-two years of age; and is still working.
She is fulfilled by working and has accomplished so many
financial goals. Her children are great stewards and are all
working tirelessly to fulfill their goals in life. My aunt is at
the point to where she does not know who to leave her
fortune to because her children do not want any of her
earthly possessions. Do not get me wrong, what my aunt is

doing is building a legacy. God's word says, **Proverbs 13:22** - A good man leaveth an inheritance to his children's children: and the wealth of the sinner is laid up for the just.

Jesus says in **John 14:12-13** "Verily, verily, I say unto you, He that believes on Me, the works that I do shall he do also; and greater works than these shall he do; because I go unto my Father, *13* And whatsoever you shall ask in my name, that will I do, that the Father may be glorified in the Son. Jesus has performed miracles, He is truth, He is about His Father's business, He is teacher, redeemer, healer, counselor, friend, strength, love, and He is everything to me. We can do all things through Christ that strengthens us. All things are possible to Him who believes. God wants to use us to do "extra-ordinary things" all it takes it faith in Him. God is well pleased when we do our best with the talents and gifts, He has given us. Whether your talent is being used as a vessel saving lives, finding a cure for a disease, counselor, educator, protector, ruler, etcetera, it takes work. Whatever you do, do it to the best of your ability so that God gets the Glory.

Reading Steve Harvey's book entitled "JUMP" he exclaims, one must take the Leap of Faith inevitably to live and not just exist. The "JUMP" requires Faith in God. We all know what Faith is. In case you do not remember, *Hebrews 11:1* Now faith is the substance of things hoped for, the evidence of things not seen. Steve Harvey further explains, "when one "JUMPS" you will not know what will occur afterwards." That is where your Faith comes in. In laymen's terms one must have Faith in what you are wanting for yourself in this life's journey and have Faith in God, He will make it happen. You notice I did not state God can make it happen, instead I stated He "will" make it happen. That statement alone is confirming FAITH! God only requires one to have FAITH of the size of a mustard seed. Do you know how small a mustard seed is? Let me explain. I wrote an Inspiration regarding FAITH and posted on Facebook a while ago. It goes as follows: *Matthew 31*

Jesus said, "Another parable put the forth unto them, saying, The kingdom of heaven is like to a grain of mustard seed, which a man took, and sowed in his field:" *32* Jesus said, "Which indeed is the least of all seeds: but when it is grown, it is the greatest among herbs, and becometh a tree, so that the birds of the air come and lodge in the branches thereof." Life is like a tree, some people are your leaves, some are branches and others are your roots. Do not let go of your roots, if sown into good ground. The mustard seed is such a small inkling. However, God requires us to have faith the size of a mustard seed. If we are smart, we would surround ourselves with people of like-minded faith. When connected we form great networks (branches) so strong and durable we will not break or disconnect. Because we (the kingdom of heaven) are rooted and sown into good ground, which also beareth fruit, and bringeth forth hundredfold, sixty and some thirty. *Matthew 13:23* Jesus said, "But he that received seed into the good ground is he that heareth the word, and understandeth it, which also beareth fruit, and bringeth forth, some a hundredfold, some sixty, some thirty." Do not fall by the wayside or stony places, be the kind of believer that bring forth fruit. *9* Who hath ears to hear, let him hear. ***Romans 10:17*** So then faith cometh by hearing, and hearing by the word of God. Your FAITH put into action is through prayer and believing God will manifest the desires of your heart. The more your FAITH grow the stronger you will become. And your relationship with God will strengthen as well.

Purpose in Life

Great vision precedes great achievement. A person without a vision is at worst, purposeless. At best, one is subject to personal – and sometimes selfish – agendas. You do not have to be the greatest visionary. But you do have to state the vision. However, you also must keep the vision in your presence and remind yourself of the progress that is being made to achieve the vision. Small achievements accomplishing short term goals should be celebrated. "The most important days in your life are the day you were born and the day you find out why." (You discover your purpose in life). Moreover, when God gives any man wealth and possessions, and enables him to enjoy them, to accept his lot and be happy in his work this is a gift of God *Ecclesiastes 5:19*. Some of us have dreams to change the world, own a business, author a book, entertain (act), and be president of the United States etcetera. We witnessed a breakthrough in our Nation's history 2020, swearing in the first woman of color as Vice President of the United States.

Whatever your dream is, I challenge you to dream and think of something so BIG that God will have to intervene to make it happen. God is a BIG God; we cannot go to Him with mediocrity. God wants more than anything to be instrumental in developing who we are and what we would like to do however it has to be according to His Will. A dream is a vision of the imagination. Remember, for every vision, God will make provision. Meaning, the Lord will make a way somehow for your dream to come true. It does not matter how big of a dream you can conjure up in your mind, nothing is too "Big" for God. God Himself is a "Big" God. Believe God for the impossible.

There are so many extremely poor to extraordinarily rich stories until I just cannot tell them all. The stories that I am sharing true however, they will inspire, motivate, and encourage you to be all God created you to be! One story that comes to mind is Nick Cannon's. Nick Cannon is a professional actor that starred on Nickelodeon Television for years. Nick Cannon had a desire to marry vocalist,

Mariah Carey. With God all things are possible. The young man eventually got who he asked for. The two were married and gave birth to twins. They are now divorced however, my point is as a child, he had a desire, fantasy, a dream to marry Mariah Carey and his dream came true.

Raven Simoné, at the mere age of two years old watched the "Cosby Show" with her parents. She informed her parents that she has a dream to act and have a role on the "Cosby Show." Her parents (believed) packed their things and moved to where the "Cosby Show" had been taping. The rest of the story is history. Little Raven Simoné dream came true and had obtained a recurring role on the "Cosby Show" as Olivia, Denise's (Lisa Bonet) stepdaughter. I do not know what denomination religiously either person belonged to however, I know what moves God. To please God, one must "have FAITH! And Believe." *Hebrews 11:6* says, "But without faith it is impossible to please him: for he, that cometh to God must believe that he is, and that he is a rewarder of them that diligently seek him." Raven Simone has gone on to grow up before our very eyes and at one point had her very own television show called, "That's so Raven." You even had a recurring role on my favorite talk show "The View."

The late great Dr. Myles Monroe's book "Living with Purpose" says "Thomas Edison was a great inventor. Many of the things we enjoy today, including the electric light, are the fruit of his willingness to be responsible for the possibilities hidden within him. He was not afraid to roll up his sleeves and work out his potential to make visible that which existed, but we could not see. His life mirrored his words:" "Genius is 1 percent inspiration and 99 percent perspiration."

James 2:17 says, Faith without works is dead. Meaning, if you have a dream, what are you going to do to keep hope alive and work towards your dream? For example: The greatest basketball player practiced basketball every chance he had, Michael Jordan is a living witness. Benjamin Franklin kept experimenting with electricity until his vision

became reality. Did you know Milton Hershey the inventor
of the luscious Hershey candy bar went broke trying to
pursue his dream and love for candy? Milton Hershey's
love for confection started at an early age and flourished
when he established The Hershey Chocolate Company in
1894. By 1900, he sold his very first candy bar. Today, his
portfolio of brands has expanded beyond the beloved and
iconic HERSHEY'S Milk Chocolate Bar. Do the math it
took Milton Hershey six years just to sell his first candy
bar! At first you fail Try, try, try again. The proverb can be
traced back to Robert the Bruce "If at first you don't
succeed try, try and try again." Robert the Bruce, king of
Scotland, is meant to have told his troops this shortly
before walloping the English at Bannockburn in 1314.

Hebrews 11:4 By Faith Able offered unto God a
more excellent sacrifice than Cain, by which he obtained
witness that he was righteous, God testifying of his gifts:
and by it he is being dead speaketh. *5* By Faith Enoch was
translated that he should not see death; and was not found,

because God had translated him: for before his translation
he had this testimony, that he pleased God. *7* by Faith
Noah, being warned of God of things not seen yet, moved
with fear, prepared an ark to the saving of his house; by the
which he condemned the world, and became heir of the
righteousness which is by Faith. By Faith Abraham, when
he was called to go out into a place which he should after
receiving for an inheritance, obeyed; and he went out, not
knowing whiter he went. *11* through Faith also Sara herself
received strength to conceive seed and was delivered of a
child when she was past age, because she judged him
faithful who had promised.

One of my all-time favorite fairy tales is
"Cinderella." Think about it, Cinderella had a tough life
without her father. He died when she was a teenager. She
had no other family other than her stepmother and
stepsisters. As story goes, her mother had passed away
when she was a child. Cinderella went through hell, but she
stayed positive and optimistic regarding life. Cinderella

was not afraid to dream. She was not fearful, to my understanding she did not fear her stepsisters or stepmother, Cinderella was just a kind-hearted person. Cinderella was a loving, caring, self-less, respectful, and considerate lady. Just when she was at her breaking point and about to give up is when the opportunity presented itself for her to meet the prince (her destiny) of the kingdom. Although evil kept getting in the way through her stepmother and stepsisters, in the end she got what she had wished and dreamed for, her prince. I must add her prince new she was his wife, the moment he laid eyes on her. Her prince found Cinderella to be his good thing. They were married and lived happily ever after.

Although the story is a fairy tale, there are real life applications from which we can learn. 1) Accept what God allows. 2) Believe and Dream BIG! 3) Destiny will find you if you are in position. You cannot be afraid to strive for something bigger and greater than your expectations. If you are going to fear someone, fear the Lord who made heaven

and earth. The Lord is a Big God therefore you must ask
him for a BIG purpose along with the desires of your heart
to happen according to His will for your life. Ask for the
BIG, the impossible in Jesus' name. Dream BIG, about
things that are bigger than yourself, so that it will take God
and no one else to allow your dreams, vision, purpose, and
plan for your life to happen. God can and will get glory out
of your life in Jesus' name Amen.

Another extremely poor to extraordinarily rich
production I find filled with optimism is "Annie." The plot
is described as "Annie" follows the story of orphan Annie,
who finds herself in the hands of billionaire "Daddy"
Warbucks after spending some time in an orphanage run by
the widely disliked Ms. Hannigan. After becoming curious
about the who and whereabouts of her birth parents,
"Daddy" Warbucks helps "Annie" search for her parents.
While searching for her parents, "Daddy" Warbucks invites
Annie to stay at his billion-dollar mansion at the cost of
helping him improve his public image. The theme of the

play and/or the overall message is having and holding hope
and optimism through life's journey, no matter what the
circumstances, is what ANNIE is all about, and what the
character of Annie symbolizes.

Fight the Good Fight of Faith

I heard someone say once, "You will never fly, if you do not jump." It takes courage to leap, jump and fly. Taking a leap of faith is "symbolic" in trusting God, to know that He is the pilot, and you are under His mighty wing. You will never understand or know who you aspire to be if you do not act. You must trust God in all that you do and in all you are. **Proverbs 3:5** Trust in the Lord with all thine heart; and lean not unto thy own understanding. **6** In all thy ways acknowledge Him, and He shall direct thy paths.

Do not be afraid of failing. Listening to Les Brown's motivational speech "You Deserve" changed my life! There are two points he brought out while speaking that stay with me to this day. 1) "The inner conversation that we have with ourselves is the reason we do not live up to our full potential. One must stop saying to oneself having the desires of one's heart is unachievable." Fear is a deterrent that some possess within, which is why one's goals cannot be reached and/or accomplished. *2 Timothy 1:7* - For God hath not given us the spirit of fear; but of power, and of love, and of a sound mind. *Hebrews 13:6* - So that we may boldly say, The Lord is my helper, and I will not fear what man shall do unto me. *Psalms 23:4* - Yes, though I walk through the valley of the shadow of death, I will fear no evil: for thou art with me; thy rod and thy staff they comfort me. *Psalms 27:1* - (A Psalm of David.) The LORD is my light and my salvation; whom shall I fear? the LORD is the strength of my life; of whom shall I be afraid? Les Brown also goes on to state that "who needs enemies when there is a fear within?" "We cannot get out of this life alive, so fear should not ever be a hinderance." 2) "The wealthiest place is the graveyard because most people die not reaching their goals, ambitions, and desires." I do not know about you, but I have desire to accomplish any and everything "GREAT" the Lord above allows for my life! It takes great courage to leap, to pursue your dreams, goals, desires, and ambitions in life. You may fail but God is never failing. It takes courage to trust the Lord with your life. God will never lead, guide, and direct you the wrong way. I often ponder if God is so good, powerful, strong, and almighty, why we have such a challenging time trusting in Him? God's word is true. All that one must do is just believe.

Take Abraham for instance. Abraham now acknowledged as the Father of All nations. Abraham trusted God so much that he was willing to sacrifice his son Isaac once God commanded him to do so. But at the very last minute as Abraham was about to sacrifice Isaac, *Genesis 22:11*"And the angel of the LORD called unto him out of heaven, and said, Abraham, Abraham: and he said, here am I." *23*"And he said, lay not thine hand upon the lad, neither do thou anything unto him: for now I know that thou fearest God, seeing thou hast not withheld thy son, thine only son from me." The word of God says this race is not given to the swift or the strong; it is given to those who endure to the end. I am reminding of some special women who I admire and who defeated the odds. They did not allow their extraordinary circumstances to defeat their goal, motivation, dreams, and aspirations in life.

Wilma Rudolph was born June 23, 1940, in Bethlehem, Tennessee, to a poor and exceptionally large family. Every circumstance was stacked against her from the day she was born. She was born prematurely at 4.5 pounds, the 20th of twenty-two siblings. Wilma contracted infantile paralysis caused by the polio virus at age four. She was a sickly child, stricken with double pneumonia, scarlet fever and polio as a child who had to wear a brace on her left leg. She overcame her disabilities through physical therapy and arduous work, becoming a gifted runner to compete in the 1956 Summer Olympic Games, and in 1960, she became the first African American woman to win three gold medals in track and field at a single Olympics.

Harriet Tubman (1832-1913) was born into slavery and badly treated as a young girl; Harriet Tubman found a shining ray of hope in the Bible stories her mother told. The account of Israel's escape from slavery under Pharaoh showed her a God who desired freedom for His people. Harriet aka "A Woman called Moses" meaning the Moses of her time exemplifying the Moses in the bible, found freedom when she slipped over the Maryland state line and out of slavery. She could not remain content, however, knowing so many were still trapped in captivity. So, she led more than a dozen rescue missions to free those still in slavery, dismissing the personal danger. "I cannot die but once," she said. Harriet knew the truth of the statement: "Do not be afraid of those who kill the body but cannot kill the soul." *Matthew 10:28*. When Harriet Tubman could not forget those still trapped in slavery, she showed us a picture of Christ, who did not forget us when we were trapped in our sins. Her courageous example inspires us to remember those who remain without hope in the world. Harriet Tubman defeated the odds when God used her to guide the path and rescue slaves to freedom. Harriet Tubman was significant abolitionist and political activist.

Oprah Winfrey born January 29, 1954, to an unwed teenage mother, she spent her first years on her grandmother's farm in Kosciusko, Mississippi, while her mother looked for work in the North. Her world changed for the worse at age six, when she was sent to Milwaukee to live with her mother, who had found work as a housecleaner. In the long days when her mother was absent from their inner-city apartment, male relatives and another visitor molested young Oprah. The abuse lasted from age nine to thirteen, was emotionally devastating. When she tried to run away, she was sent to a juvenile detention home, only to be denied admission because all the beds were filled. At age fourteen she was out of the house and on her own. By her own account she was sexually promiscuous as a teenager. After giving birth to a baby boy who died in infancy, she went to Nashville, Tennessee to live with her father.

At age 17, Oprah Winfrey won the Miss Black Tennessee beauty pageant and was offered an on-air job at

WVOL, a radio station serving the African American community in Nashville. In 1976, she moved to Baltimore to join WJZ-TV News as a co-anchor. There, she hosted her first talk show, "People Are Talking," while continuing to serve as anchor and news reporter. A year later, Oprah Winfrey defeated the odds when the "The Oprah Winfrey Show" was broadcast nationally, and quickly became the number one talk show in national syndication. God has used Oprah and opened doors for her that is unimaginable. One of Oprah's quotes is "Create the highest grandest vision possible for your life, because you become what you believe." (Oprah Winfrey). I would like to add with God nothing is impossible. Now billionaire, she is best known for hosting her own internationally popular talk show from 1986-2011. She is an actor, philanthropist, publisher, and producer. Her latest accomplishment is establishing her "OWN" television network which O.W.N. "Oprah Winfrey Network."

Now there are some millionaires I admire who are men too! Steve Harvey for one. Mr. Harvey's story is so motivating and so full of FAITH, I just had to mention. Mr. Harvey's story reminds of the scripture, **James 2:18** Yea, a man may say, thou hast faith, and I have works shew me thy faith without thy works, and I will shew thee my faith by my works. The road to success was not an easy one. It left Mr. Harvey homeless, living in his car and traveling the country for performances. In 1990, he won a national comedy competition which led to his big break on Showtime at the Apollo. From that moment on, Mr. Harvey's career took off. Steve Harvey's entry into comedy was a leap of faith. He was encouraged to perform at an open mic comedy night in 1985. Mr. Harvey brought down the house, and the next day he quit his job to pursue his dream. As Mr. Harvey says, "You have to jump and take a leap of faith in order to soar." Mr. Harvey is one of the most recognizable and sought-after celebrities in the world. His relatable, honest, and inspiring personality has made

him one of the most trusted personalities in media.
178,000,000 US viewers welcome Steve Harvey into their
homes on a yearly basis—that is over 55% of the total U.S.
population. Mr. Harvey began his radio career in 2000. His
show, The Steve Harvey Morning Show, airs on more than
one hundred radio stations nationally and reaches over six
million weekly listeners. The Steve Harvey Morning Show
is the most listened to syndicated morning show in
America. In addition to his wide-ranging accomplishments
as an entertainer, Mr. Harvey is also a best-selling author.
Mr. Harvey has received accolades throughout his career.
He received 14 Daytime Emmy nominations resulting in
six Daytime Emmy Awards. Harvey was also nominated
for one Primetime Emmy as the host of Little Big Shots. In
addition to his Emmys, Mr. Harvey has received 10
NAACP Image Awards and a total of 14 nominations.
Today Steve Harvey remains known as the busiest man in
Hollywood. But in addition to his work on screen, radio,

stage and print, Harvey is a resolute mentor and an inspiring motivator to his fans.

Let me not forget Tyler Perry, Billionaire Extraordinaire. Tyler Perry's journey to me is more like a testament of FAITH! Mr. Perry's testimony reminds me of the scripture, **Hebrews 11:16** But without faith it is impossible to please him: for he, that cometh to God must believe that he is, and that he is a rewarder of them that diligently seek him. The mastermind behind 17 feature films, 20 stage plays, seven television shows, a New York Times bestselling book, Tyler has built an empire that has attracted audiences and built communities, from the Tyler Perry Studios home base in Atlanta, Georgia, throughout the world. Celebrated "among the pantheon of today's greatest cinematic innovators," his unique blend of spiritual hope and down-home humor continues to shape his inspiring life story, connecting with fans across the globe and always leaving space to dream. Tyler's legacy is the modern epitome of the American dream. Born and raised in

New Orleans, his childhood was marked by poverty and a household scarred by abuse. From an early age, Tyler learned to write down his daily thoughts and experiences in a series of soul-searching letters to himself – advice he gleaned from Oprah Winfrey that set his career in motion. Characterized by strength, faith, and determination during a turbulent adolescence, these letters provided Tyler with the inspiration to delve into writing his first play, I Know I have Been Changed in 1992. Saving every dollar, Tyler staged the play for what he hoped would be a packed audience, but the seats remained empty. Never would he have imagined that six years later, that same play would sell out a local run, forcing the production to move to the acclaimed Fox Theatre in Atlanta, or that in 2015, his original play, Madea on the Run, would be sold out in theaters nationwide. Not one to rest on his successes, in 2015 Tyler Perry Studios announced plans to expand operations in Atlanta with the acquisition of Fort McPherson. The studio, which was already home to the production of over fifteen films and almost eight hundred episodes of Tyler's five television series, has now made a home on over 330 acres. With that, Tyler Perry Studios welcomes more than four hundred job opportunities to the Atlanta community across Tyler's productions, as well as major feature films and television shows.

Dr. Martin Luther King Jr. his legacy will live on forever! Dr. King Jr.'s journey is the epitome of the scripture 2 Corinthians 5:7 says we walk by Faith and not by sight. Meaning, we do not believe on the visible, looks can be deceiving. Dr. Martin Luther King Jr. had a dream of "equality" for all men. He kept the FAITH in God and believed God for what he believed would come true. We are all living witnesses of Dr. Martin Luther King's dream and legacy. Although he did not have an opportunity to visually see things as they are now, I am almost certain God showed him the vision of things as we live it today. God used Dr. Martin Luther King Jr. as His vessel to fulfill a vision and dream that is "extra-ordinary." And the dream and legacy will live on forever. We must learn to speak things into existence. Speak and believe on things (dreams) as though they were. *Hebrews 11:1* says Faith is the substance of things hoped for and the evidence of things not seen. Unfortunately, Dr. King did not live to see his dream manifested. However, I do believe God showed him in his dreams. It is my belief that is the reason Dr. King was able to speak so eloquently in his "I have a DREAM" speech. Dr. King spoke as if he had seen the Glory of the Lord. As he put it, He had seen the "Promised Land" and He had been to the "Mountain Top." He also stated, "he may not get there with us." That is FAITH in God at its finest!

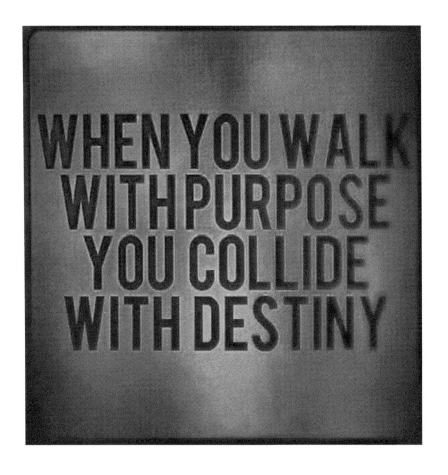

Purpose in Marriage

In my first book "Journey into Singleness Live a
Life of Joy Fulfillment and Contentment" I stress on the
Joy, Fulfillment, and Contentment of being "single." When
God makes you whole, meaning one does not desire
anything but God's will for your life, God truly has your
heart, mind, body, and spirit, you will be ready for God to
present you with a mate. The belief that a romantic partner
"completes" us is now part of popular culture. But it is
true? Many married couples still feel incomplete because
they have not been able to have children and others who
have kids feel something else is missing. No human can
fully complete us. Apostle Paul gives another solution. In
Colossians 2:9-10 "For in Christ lives all the fullness of
God in a human body. So, you are complete through your
union with Christ." Jesus does not just forgive us and
liberate us; He completes us by bringing the life of God
into our lives. Marriage is good, but it cannot make us
whole. Only Jesus can do that. Instead of expecting a

person, career, or anything else to complete us, let us accept God's invitation to let His fullness fill our lives more. Until then, you are not ready. The same thing applies to the people, except with men the difference is you will know her when you see her. ***Proverbs 18:22*** - Whoso findeth a wife findeth a good thing, and obtaineth favour of the LORD. God inputs in a man's spirit who his wife is at times when he first lays his eyes on her. You will be attracted to her spirit. You will not be able to stop thinking about her. You will be someone she needs in her life not particularly someone whom she wants or desires. She will not know that she needs you because she will be so consumed in doing the Lord's work and focused on His will for her life. She will be content, fulfilled, and enthusiastic about her life's works. She may even reject you at first but keep the faith in God. The same goes for you, do not settle for anything less than your self-worth.

I know a couple who met for the first time in college. When the man first saw her, he knew she was his wife. They eventually became friends however when the man told the woman, she was his wife, the woman rejected him. They went on to graduate college, obtained great careers within their fields, the entire time they remained friends. The man continued to keep his desire alive by building a foundation for the entire time she rejected him. He prayed and remained faithful to God. He had them a house built. He saved money and continued to woo this woman until finally, he asked her to marry him again. For some reason this time, the woman said, "Something came over her unto the point, she could not say no to him any longer." She said, "Yes." What I like about their story is the entire time they were engaged, the man never told his wife, he had them a house built. After they returned from their honeymoon, they drove up in the driveway to their new home. It was not until he picked her up and carried her over the threshold, he announced that she was home. This was about ten years ago. To date they are happily married, serving God together with three beautiful children. Again, men who find their wives find a good thing and obtain favor with God.

It is my belief that one should be completely alone before marriage is even a possibility. You should not want anyone to complete you. A mate comes only to enhance who you already are in Christ. You both must still live single, individualized, and whole lives married but as one. I challenge you to dream and dream big! God is a big God. To really get God's attention you must ask Him for big desires, goals, dreams, and ambitions in life. You should not want something easily given. You should desire something so huge and big in life that it will take God and God alone to open doors so that you can accomplish it.

Do not ever judge a book by its cover. Remember God will give you just what you need, just when you need it. Let me add, the Lord knows us better than we know ourselves. God knew us and predestined us to be who we are before we ever conceived. Let me explain, I missed a good man back in 2007-2008. Right after I broke up with my friend who was married but eventually died, I was reunited with an old acquaintance. I had known him around ten years or so but never showed any interest in him because in my mind he did not look like what I imagined the man I wanted for myself. To add insult to injury, God kept giving me sound confirmation that he was the one for me. This transpired back in 1997. Ten years later the opportunity had been presented again for us to date one another. For some reason this time, he would not take no for an answer. We met at church in 1997. Everyone at the church including his father was on board and cheering us on to date. My children even liked the man. I had even been fasting and praying for a husband back then. God had even showed me in a dream the man of God he had for me was wearing a blue suit. I could not see his face but for several weeks straight the gentlemen at church wore a navy-blue suit identical to the man in my dream. All I had to do was trust God instead I leaned to my own understanding.

So, eventually we went out on a date in 2007. I had never had so much fun, excitement and enjoyment on a date with anyone. He turned out to be just who I always wanted. We laughed, prayed together, danced, played games together, went to church and talked on the phone when we could not go out on dates. We were inseparable for an entire year. This time around, things were so different because during the time he left the church and moved out of state, I had no idea that he had gotten married, had children, and divorced during the period of 1997-2007. He was now obligated to his children. As a result, he had to spend countless weeks and months in and out of town where the children resided. His children at the time were two and three. He wanted us to get married, but I did not want all the baby mama drama in my life. He asked me to wait on him and once he returned a year later, he wanted us to get married. I just did not want to go through all the drama. I waited on him for a year but when he returned, I had changed. By then my friend had died and I had changed my place of worship. Everything was so different. We eventually went our separate ways.

From what I have heard, this gentleman went on with his life, got married in 2010 and moved to New England. As for me, God is in control. Mind you, when God was trying to bring us together as spouses, this man had never been married, he was single and had only one daughter who just happened to be my eldest daughter's age at the time, which was twelve or thirteen. I did not receive him, when I should have. Similarly, he pursued me repeatedly until he gave up and sought interest in someone else. I have learned never to judge a book by its cover; you just might miss a blessing. God is a God of His word; He is His word. God is full of honesty and integrity. God will always come through for you. He may not come when you want Him, but He is always on time. God has a profound sense of humor at times. He will show us what we missed had we been obedient. It is my belief that is what is meant by the old cliché the Lord will give and the Lord will take away. Obedience does out way sacrifice anytime, anyway and any day.

I remember two stories that recall the first one in **Genesis 34.** Jacob and Leah's daughter Dinah when she was seen by Shechem the son of Ha'mor the Hivite, prince of the country, saw her; he took her and lay with her, and defiled her. Jacob's sons were so grieved, and they were terribly angry, because he had brought foolishness into Israel by lying with their sister which ought not to have been done. Although Shechem soul cleaved to Dinah's, he loved her and spoke kindly of her, he went about things the wrong way. In this day and time what Shechem did to Dinah is considered rape. Shechem wanted to marry Dinah. The sons of Jacob, Dinah's brothers did not want to allow their sister to be given to for one who had committed such a heinous act and was uncircumcised. The bible says they (the brothers) deceitfully consented to giving their sister if every male in Shechem village be circumcised. The villagers eventually agreed to get circumcised. It was a

trick because on the third day when everyone was sore and
could not protect their selves, the sons of Jacob, Simeon
and Levi, Dinah's brothers, took each man his sword, and
came upon the city boldly, and slew all the males. They
also slew Ha'mor and Shechem his son with the edge of the
sword, and took Dinah out of Shechem house, and went
out. The brothers after taking their sister back took their
sheep, and their oxen, and their asses, and that which was
in the city, and that which was in the field. And all their
wealth, and all their little ones, and their wives took them
captive, and overindulged even all that was in the house.

My point is this: For a man to lay with a woman
that he is not married to is serious business, so serious back
then that the brothers did not comprehend how to deal with
their sister being taken in that manner. They considered
their sister as being a harlot. The brothers killed an entire
village of people. In their minds they wanted to make their
sister righteous again and, in their eyesight, they took it
upon themselves to kill an entire village.   It is

ridiculous to me that couples are experiencing pre-marital sex anyway. Back in the day, pre-marital sex was not to be tolerated. Parents taught their children to keep themselves until marriage. In the bible days a woman was considered unclean, a harlot, Jezebel if found guilty of the act of fornication and/or adultery. The act could cost them their life. It is ridiculous to me that couples are experiencing pre-marital sex anyway. Back in the day, pre-marital sex was not to be tolerated. Parents taught their children to keep themselves until marriage. The other story is in *John 8* when Jesus was teaching in the temple. The scribes and Pharisees brought unto Him a woman taken in adultery; and when they had set her in the midst, they said to Jesus, "Master this woman was taken in adultery in the very act." They told Jesus the Law of Moses commanded them to stone her. This is when Jesus stooped down and with His finger wrote on the ground, as though he did not hear them. They continued to ask Him, Jesus eventually lifted His head and said to them "He that is without sin among you, let him first cast a stone at her." They were all convicted starting with the eldest. One by one they left. Jesus told the woman, "Neither do I condemn thee: go, and sin no more." The sin of adultery back in the bible days in found guilty, was death. We must remember God is same God today, yesterday, and forever. The sin of adultery is in fact one of the Ten Commandments. This sin of adultery is a horrendous act. God still judges.

Julie Schwab, Discovery Series Author writes "Love is as strong as death, it's jealousy unyielding as the grave." "Comparing graves and death odd but they are strong because they do not give up their captives. However, neither will true love give up the loved one." Throughout the Bible, the love of spouses is compared to God's love. *Ephesians 5:25* Husbands, love your wives, even as Christ also loved the church, and gave himself for it; *Isaiah 54:5* For thy Maker is thine husband; the LORD of hosts is his name; and thy Redeemer the Holy One of Israel; The God of the whole earth shall be called. *Revelation 21:2* And I

John saw the holy city, new Jerusalem, coming down from
God out of heaven, prepared as a bride adorned for her
husband.

Pursuit to Happiness in the Pursuit of Happiness

When you look in the mirror who and what do you see? When you look in the mirror do you say to yourself as WOW, I look good, or do you even look at yourself in the mirror? When I look in the mirror, I say to myself I wish I could get rid of this belly fat. But I am loving everything else I see. Now, what do you think God sees when He searches your heart? Will God say, WOW! I like what I see, or will He say, I wish he/she will get rid of

_____. In the movie "Pursuit to Happiness" Will Smith's character Chris would watch people as if he is moving in slow motion because, they all from his perspective seemed happy. By the end of the movie, which it is the true story of Chris Gardner, now multi-millionaire, Chris had found "his" happiness. Notice I stated "his" happiness because everyone's views of happiness are different. Chris Gardner's character found primarily a peace within, next he found his purpose – (something set up as an object or end to be attained). Lastly, he was able to obtain prosperity.

The pursuit of happiness is defined as a fundamental right mentioned in the Declaration of Independence to freely pursue joy and live life in a way that makes you happy if you do not do anything illegal or violate the rights of others. This statement means that we have the right to be free and live life happy! Is not that good news? Although the world has their definition of happiness, we as Christians are free indeed because the son has set us free. We are free to live a life of joy this world did not give to us, and this world cannot take away. We are free because the Blood of the Lamb have redeemed us. We are free to live a life in a way that makes us happy because the joy of the Lord is our strength. We are free and made whole again because we are new creatures in Christ. Jesus came that we may have life and life more abundantly. What exactly does that mean for Christians (believers)? It means that we can have heaven on earth. God placed the desire for a full life in every human being, and He longs for people to experience a loving relationship with Him. But he also warned them that the "thief" would use people, things, and circumstances to attempt to ravage their lives. The claims each made to give life would be counterfeit and an imitation. In contrast, Jesus's offer is what is true, "eternal life" and the promise that "no one will snatch us out of His hand." The abundance means AFFLUENCE, WEALTH per the Webster's dictionary. So, if Jesus came that we may have life and life affluence and wealthy than we should. Only Jesus can fill the empty spaces in our hearts with life. If you are feeling empty, call out to Him today. And if you are experiencing serious struggles, seek out godly counsel. Christ alone provides life that is abundant and full, life full of meaning found in Him. But the question is what is your meaning of happiness? How do you get to your happiness? The pursuit to happiness as it pertains to the science of happiness suggests the seven habits of happy people. 1) Express your heart. People who have one or more close friendships are happier. It does not seem to matter if we have a large network of close relationships or not. What seems to be effective is if and how often we cooperate in activities and share our personal feelings with a friend or relative. "Active-constructive responding," which is the ability to express genuine interest in what people say, and respond in encouraging ways, is a powerful way to enrich relationships and cultivate positive emotions. 2) Cultivate kindness. People who volunteer or simply care for others on a consistent basis seem to be happier and less depressed. Although "caring" can involve volunteering as part of an organized group or club, it can be as simple as reaching out to a colleague or classmate who looks lonely or is struggling with an issue. 3) Keep moving and eat well. Regular exercise has been associated with improved mental well-being and a lower incidence of depression. The Cochrane Review (the most influential medical review of its kind in the world) has produced a landmark analysis of 23 studies on exercise and depression. One of the major conclusions was that exercise had a "large clinical impact" on depression. Many studies are proving the ancient adage, "sound body, sound mind," including the recent discovery of a "gut-brain axis," psych biotics, and a link between excessive sugar consumption and depression. 4) Find your flow. If we are deeply involved in trying to reach a goal, or an activity that is challenging but well suited to our skills, we experience a joyful state called "flow." Many kinds of activities, such as sports, playing an instrument, or teaching, can produce the experience a joyful state called "flow." Many kinds of activities, such as sports, playing an instrument, or teaching, can produce the experience of flow. According to Mihaly Csikszentmihalyi, a pioneer of the scientific study of happiness, flow is a type of intrinsic motivation. In his words, "you do what you're doing primarily because you like what you're doing. If you learn only for external, extrinsic reason, you will forget it as soon as you are no longer forced to remember what you want to do. 5) Discovering Meaning. Studies demonstrate a close link between spiritual and religious practice and happiness. Spirituality is closely related to the discovery of greater meaning in our lives. As the psychologist Martin Seligman emphasizes, through the meaningful life we discover a deeper kind of happiness…6) Discover and use your strengths. Studies by experts such as Martin Seligman in the new field of Positive Psychology show that the happiest people are those that have discovered their unique strengths (such as persistence and critical thinking) and virtues (such as humanity) and use those strengths and virtues for a purpose that is greater than their own personal goals (Authentic Happiness: Using the New Positive Psychology to Realize Your Potential for Lasting Fulfillment). 7) Treasure gratitude, mindfulness, and hope. Of all the areas studied in the young field of positive psychology, gratitude has received the most attention. Grateful people have shown to have greater positive emotion, a greater sense of belonging, and lower incidence of depression and stress.

Pursuit to happiness as it pertains to the emotions of happiness is a conscious effort. Happiness does not fall from the sky. Happiness is pursued daily. The happiness you made or had the day before is a memory. Each day is a different pursuit of happiness because each day is new. Happiness can be defined as a pleasurable or satisfying experience. I might add it is temporary unless pursued daily. "Happiness is the meaning and the purpose of life, the whole aim and end of human existence." – Aristotle There are levels of happiness from my perspective and experience of happiness entails: But first one must acknowledge nothing, or no one is perfect. And as stated previously, money does not make you happy, neither can anyone else. First, there is an experience of happiness being happy for others. To be happy for others, you must be happy with self because haters are real. A hater is envious or jealous of you as a person and/or what you have i.e., prestige, intelligence, education, material possessions, money, fame, joy etcetera. Second, there is an experience of happiness of achievement, accomplishment such as an earned degree, homeownership, business ownership. Lastly, there is an experience of happiness within that stems from your relationship with God. This happiness called joy does not come from material possessions or temporal things. This joy comes from a PEACE only God can give. In pursuit of peace, one must acknowledge God is Lord. Acceptance of Jesus Christ as Lord and Savior. Our goal while on earth is to become like and/or emulate Jesus. Here is also an experience of happiness that comes through service. When supporting others, giving to others, serving others, it feels good to give. Serving gives you a sense of belonging and purpose by filling a void in your life. It is a blessing to be on the giving side because you have it to give. Whether you are giving your time or money. Even if you do not have money to give, you have your talents and gifts to give. One must be at peace before one can pursuit purpose and prosperity. Again, true joy and happiness derives from a peace within that only comes from a

relationship with God. Dr. Tal Ben Shahar, Harvard
Professor teaches the largest course –

Six Tips of Happiness

1) Give yourself permission to be human. When we
accept emotions such as fear, sadness, frustration, anger
etcetera, go through the emotion. 2) Happiness is the
overall experience of pleasure and meaning. Whether at
work or at home, the goal is to engage in activities that are
both personally significant and enjoyable. Nobody really
cares if you are miserable so you might as well be happy.
3) Happiness is mostly dependent on our state of mind not
on our status or the state of our bank account. Barring
extreme circumstances, our level of well-being is
determined by what we choose to focus on and by our
interpretation of external events. 4) Simplify – We are too
busy trying to squeeze in more activities into less and less
time. Quantity influences quality, and we compromise on
our happiness by trying to do too much. 5) Remember the
mind body connection. Meditation is a fantastic way to be

in tune body – spirit – mind – balance. 6) Express gratitude whenever possible. Mediation is considered an exercise during which the individual enters an extended state of contemplation and reflection over a specific subject or their general existence, sometimes with a view to attain a differing state of consciousness per the Psychology Dictionary. Start by taking 2 to 3 deep breaths when entering your quiet place. This is a time when you can be as vulnerable as need be. A time when you can cry, scream, and shout. Get everything out. Think about whenever a storm comes there is the rain, wind, thunder, and lighting. After the storm there is a sense of cleansing, peace, and serenity. Kneel to pray and just tell God all about it.

While in complete silence connect with your core consciousness and your deepest self. This is the mainstream as to how to hear from God. That silence is the source of creativity, love compassion, joy, and peace. Who you are is not your assumed identity but consciousness that it is always a sea of infinite possibilities? Consciousness transcends time and because it is not in time, cannot be destroyed. That is your true self. You cannot be in touch with your soul unless you get past the noise that your mind produces such as worry, stress, job related issues, family drama etcetera. Once you have overcome that noise, you are in touch with the source which is God. God is the source of everything. Some people call being in touch with God the infinite consciousness or the unlimited spirit. I call it the "Holy Spirit" It does not matter which name you use. That connection can only come through in silence and prayer.

"Stop looking
for
Happiness in
the
Same place you
lost it."

Deepak Chopra says, "Trade multitasking for focus." "Mindfulness creates centered awareness. When you do one thing at a time, you are guaranteed excellent results." This in turn can become difficult for some women. It is a woman's nature to multi-task. Some of us do not feel normal doing one thing at a time however this is the natural functioning of the mind. "Keep a separate time for daily meditation, exercise, relationships, work and relaxation. Do not mix them." Set a time to complete each task. I like to use a daily calendar or log sheet kept handy. Sticky notes are another wonderful way to keep up with all your daily tasks. Post the stick notes on things you must eventually use such as the refrigerator, bathroom mirror and or bedroom mirror. Use your handy mobile device to schedule your tasks. The remarkable thing about the mobile device is you can set reminders to be alerted to maintain your daily activities. It is okay to schedule time for relationships and for the same reason it is okay to set time just for you. "Remember if you do too many things

simultaneously, it messes up your neural circuits. Your
conscious brain should only focus on one thing at a time."
The main thing to do at times is meditate. Whether you
meditate in the morning or at the end of the day, this is a
time to relax in silence and hear from God. We too often
take our live for granted. Keep in mind: Life is not fair; it is
still good! Envy is a waste of time. You already have all
you need. You can get through anything if you stay put in
today, no one oversees your happiness except you.
Whatever does not kill you really does make you stronger.
Forgive everyone everything! However good or unpleasant
situation is it will change. You do not have to win every
argument. Agree to disagree. Time heals everything, time,
time, time. If all through our problems in a pile and saw
everyone else's we would grab our back. Do not take
yourself so seriously, No one else does. Do not compare
your life to others. You have no idea what their journey is
all about. It is never too late to have a happy childhood. But
the second one is up to you and no one else. Frame every

so-called disaster with these words: "In five years, will this
matter?"

CHAPTER 3

Pursuit a Life of Prosperity

Financial Management is important because the Lord entrusts us with what belongs to Him. Being a good steward of God's belongings is an important responsibility because trust is involved. God is the creator of everything and again everything belongs to Him. One must believe and trust God with everything and through it all. *Proverbs 3:5-6* says: Trust God with all of thine heart. Lean not unto thy own understanding. In all thine ways acknowledge Him, and He will direct thy path.

A steward is a trustee, a chief servant of God. In *James 1:17* says every good gift and every perfect gift is from above, and come down from the Father of lights, which who is no variableness, neither shadow of turning. Meaning, a man cannot receive anything except it be given from heaven. Finances are monetary resources or revenue. There are several scriptures regarding financial prosperity. *3 John 1:2* Beloved, I wish above all things that thou may prosper and be in health, even as thy soul prospers. According to *Mark 11:23* Jesus said: "For verily I say unto you that whosoever shall say unto this mountain, be thou removed, and be cast in the sea; and shall not doubt in his heart but shall believe that those things which he said shall come to pass; he shall have whatsoever he said." Does God want His children to prosper? Yes! God wants nothing more than for His children to have life and life more abundantly.

Solomon was the wisest and richest man that ever lived. Solomon understood the principles of prosperity. His proverbs revealed many truths regarding finances. There are three fundamental principles that Solomon understood that moved God to bless him financially. They are 1) Thankfulness 2) Giving and 3) Remember it is God that gives you power to get wealth.

Thankfulness Remember to thank God for everything especially for the trivial things; the mere things we often take for granted. *Ephesians 5:20* says give thanks always for all things unto God and the Father in the name of our Lord Jesus Christ. I will always bless the Lord: His praise shall continually be in my mouth. *Psalm 34:1*

Giving He who gives to the poor will not want, but he who hides his eyes will have many a curse. *Proverbs 28:27*. There is a song I often sing called "you can't beat God's given, no matter how you try. The more you give, he gives to you...." When you give, it does come back to you just like karma does. What you give may not come back to you in the same measure you gave, but it will come back. When the Lord speaks to your heart to give, give! *Proverbs 3:9-10* Honor the Lord with thy substance, and with the first fruits of all thine increase: so, thy barns filled with plenty, and thy presses shall burst forth with new wine.

I remember when I first started tithing. I had a discussion with a co-worker at work one day. I did not understand why and how she could just make out a check to her church before she spent any of her money. She tried desperately to make me understand that everything belonged to God and God required ten percent of all of thine increase. I was below a babe in Christ back then. I was just a bench on looker. Meaning I was just going to church, the word was not penetrating within me yet. One Sunday, I had gone to church and forgot to get change for offering. I only had a ten-dollar bill. I heard God say, give that! Out of obedience, I gave it. It turned out I had one of the best weeks of my life because if felt good to give. I could not wait to get paid again so that I could start tithing my gross earnings. I was raising four children at the time, single and with only one income. The Lord always came through and made a way out of no way for us once I started giving. God also requires that we give not grudgingly or out of necessity: for God loves a cheerful giver *2 Corinthians 9:7.*

Remember it is God that gives power and wealth Solomon's motive of his heart was pure and that is to bless others and establish God's covenant. You cannot be greedy and truly prosper. There is nothing wrong with wanting to have abundance for yourself and your family but giving to God and being generous to others is part of the spiritual law. Another form of giving is called sowing seeds. Whatever endeavor, vision or plan God has giving you, sow into someone who is already walking in purpose. Let me explain, I know an author personally, each time I encounter this author, if he is out promoting his book, he does not have to ask me anymore to purchase his book, he knows I will always sow into his ministry. There are various authors whom I have been following for years and each time they publish a new book, I purchase it.

My point is this: You sow seeds into people who are purposefully living as you would desire. It was never my intention on becoming an author however it is God's will. My father instilled reading in us. Reading will take you places within your mind for whatever reason you could never experience or imagine. "The more you know the more you grow." You will reap what you sow. *2 Corinthians 9:16* says, but this I say, he which soweth sparingly shall reap also sparingly, and he which soweth bountifully shall reap also bountifully. The scripture means, you sow small you reap small however if you sow great, you reap greatness.

Doing my days of Substitute teaching, to motivate the seventh-grade students, I talked then about a student my eldest daughter went to school with. From the time they entered the ninth grade until their senior year in high school, the young man asked each of his classmates for a dollar on average each day. One dollar does not seem like a lot of money, however if there are thirty students per class and there are seven periods of thirty students in each class period, do the math. I will do the math for you. The student collected an average of 105 dollars per day times five days a week times four weeks times ten months out of a year…totaling on average twenty-one thousand dollars per school year. Not to mention there were three years of his daily pursuit of prosperity. The young man on graduation day collected sixty-three thousand dollars. From what I have been told, the young man presently is extraordinarily successful and is in business for himself. The young man saw an opportunity, acted on the opportunity, and benefited from the opportunity. The bible tells us in *Matthew 7:7* to Ask, and it shall be given you; seek, and ye shall find; knock, and it shall be opened unto you:

Jesus came that we may have life and life more abundantly. *John 10:10* The thief cometh not, but for to steal, and to kill, and to destroy I am come that they might have life, and that they might have it more abundantly. Reading the scripture "may" is a key word. Jesus knew some would have the spirit of unbelief, walk in doubt and not by faith and others simply will not ask for what they want. A wise person does not live in the now but the know. Meaning applied knowledge equates to wisdom. A wise person plans, future generations. A wise person will plan, prepare, and live a prosperous life. And ensure future generations will benefit as well.

There are people
So poor
that
the only
thing they have is
money.

The Secret to Reciprocity in Giving

Al Herron, "The Working Man & Woman's Guide
to Becoming a Millionaire" reiterates "never run out of
money." Mr. Herron developed 13 Steps to becoming
financially secure. **1)** Build on a Foundation of Learning –
The first step is to build your life on a learning foundation.
You should learn to love and appreciate learning, because it
is crucial to finding your way to financial freedom. Never
shy away from an opportunity to gain experience
something of value. Be a sponge for information. Learning
is not painful; it is something you can enjoy. Begin to
cherish knowledge, so that you can use it to help yourself
ore in all aspects of your life. **2)** Put Your Savings on
Cruise Control – Putting your savings program on "cruise
control" allows you to begin seeing your way clear to
realizing true financial freedom. When you put your
savings on cruise control, your financial independence will
move closer and closer to you – and not farther and farther
away, as will happen without a good savings plan. Using

cruise control, you will have money to make investments, if you continue to save. **3)** Develop a cheerful outlook about work. Learn to be enthusiastic. Learn to "sell" yourself and your skills and services expertly, every day, at the job you have now. Become enthusiastic about yourself, your health, your family, your life, your job and/or business, and your future. **4)** Control Your Expenses – Just as you can learn to develop a habit of saving money, you can also learn to watch with great care how you spend it. You must introduce discipline into your spending routine if you expect to become a millionaire. **5)** Establish Good Credit – This step is a bridge. It lies between your old habits and your new possibilities. The good news is that even if your credit has suffered in the past, you can still redeem it. You must begin today, right now. And you must stay the course. Once you do this, you are creating a bridge from your old lifestyle to your new lifestyle – the one leading you to the financial independence you want, need, and deserve.

FORMULA for SAVINGS:

1) Save one-tenth of your income 10%

2) Give on-tenth to charity 10%

3) Pay your creditors four-tenths of your income
    40%

4) Live on four-tenths of your income 40%

    TOTAL 100%

THE ONLY THING WORSE THAN BEING BLIND IS HAVING SIGHT BUT NO VISION

-Helen Keller

6) Becoming a Homeowner is one of the best investments you can make. Owning your own home is a vital part of the "millionaire mindset." If you have a job - a steady income stream, there is no good reason you should not own your own home. Begin making movement toward ownership. Make an action plan., complete with steps and dates will help make your plan real. Home ownership is going to give you needed control over your finances and you will have more control over your inner sanctum. Controlling your inner sanctum means the possibility of ore contentment and peace in your immediate environment, enabling you to spend more quality time contemplating and considering wealth-building opportunities such as those you will learn about in this book. Finally, going through the "process" involved in purchasing a home will educate you in financial matters, and your new-found learning will render you better prepared, intellectually, to seek the financial freedom you will need on the way to becoming a millionaire. **7)** Insurance is the way you are going to protect your dream.

And while I hope and pray that God will grant you long life, if He decides to call you home before all your earthly dreams are realize, you should make sure your family will get a chance to enjoy what you have been working to achieve. Protecting your dream will also help you enjoy more financial freedom while you are living and breathing. Insurance has many functions, and many possibilities. Developing a positive and initiative-taking attitude about insurance is part of the "millionaire mindset." 8) Investing to Keep Your Money Growing – Have you heard the stories about all the lottery winners who have ended up broke? Do you ever wonder how this happens; when someone is given all the money he or she could ever need to live comfortably, never needing to work again. Instead of looking for ways to keep their money growing, they spend, spend, spent, and spend, until they have spent themselves into the poorhouse. While it is true that spending money is a necessary part of making money, spending for the sake of accumulating more material things that have little or no lasting value is not going to make anyone rich. Investing is the way to make money, and plan calls for you to invest some of your income in financially responsible and sound ways. 9) Share your wealth – One vital part of the millionaire mindset to develop a spirit of giving. It is better to give than to receive. Most of the time, we think of giving as being the opposite of getting but is getting because as being the opposite of getting but giving is getting because whenever you give away something of value, you are always going to get something of value in return. It may not be measurable in terms of dollars and cents, but – unbelievably, the most valuable things in life are not, because they are priceless.

10) Plan to Leave a Legacy – Your assets might include:

➢ Individual property such as cash, furniture, jewelry etc.
➢ Real Property such as home, apartment building, other real estate
➢ Insurance – (all insurance types)
➢ Business such as corporation, sole proprietorship, partnership
➢ Benefits such as pensions, social security

How to Start a Small Business

Getting Started Entrepreneurship is another terrific way to invest. Starting and managing a business takes motivation, desire, and talent. It also takes vision, research, and planning. Like a chess game, success in small business starts with decisive and correct opening moves. And although initial mistakes are not fatal, it takes skill, discipline, and demanding work to regain the advantage. To increase your chances for success, take the time up front to explore and evaluate your business and personal goals. Then use this information to build a comprehensive and well-thought-out business plan that will help you reach your goals. The process of developing a business plan will help you think through some principal issues that you may not have considered yet. Your plan will become a valuable tool as you set out to raise money for your business. It should also provide milestones to gauge your success.

Before starting out, list your reasons for wanting to go into business. Some of the most common reasons for starting a business are:

- ➤ You want to be your own boss.
- ➤ You want financial independence.
- ➤ You want creative freedom.
- ➤ You want to fully use your skills and knowledge.

Next you need to determine what business is right for you. "Ask yourself these questions:

- ➤ What do I like to do with my time?
- ➤ What technical skills have I learned or developed?
- ➤ What do others say I am good at?
- ➤ Will I have the support of my family?
- ➤ How much time do I have to run a successful business?
- ➤ Do I have any hobbies or interests that are marketable?

When you should identify the niche, your business will fill. Conduct the necessary research and answer these questions?

- ➤ What business am I interested in starting?
- ➤ What services or products will I sell?

> ➤ Is my idea practical, and will it fill a need?
> ➤ What is my competition?
> ➤ What is mu business's advantage over existing firms?
> ➤ Can I deliver a better-quality service?
> ➤ Can I create a demand for my business?

The ultimate step before developing your plan is the pre-business checklist. You should answer these questions:

> ➤ What skills and experience do I bring to the business?
> ➤ What will be my legal structure?
> ➤ How will my company's business records be maintained?
> ➤ What insurance coverage will be needed?
> ➤ What equipment or supplies will I need?
> ➤ How will I compensate myself?
> ➤ What are my resources?
> ➤ What financing will I need?
> ➤ Where will my business be located?
> ➤ What will I name my business?

Your answers will help you create a focused, well-researched business plan that should serve as a blueprint. It should detail how the business will be operated, managed, and capitalized. The following outline of a typical business plan can serve as a guide, but you should adapt it to your specific business. We recommend that you break down the plan into several components. This allows you to work on several sections at a time.

Marketing Strategy

- ➢ Discuss the products/services offered.
- ➢ Identify the customer demand for your product/service.
- ➢ Identify your market, its size, and locations.
- ➢ Explain how your product/service will be advertised and marketed.
- ➢ Explain the pricing strategy.

Financial Management

- ➢ Explain the source and amount of initial equity capital.
- ➢ Develop a monthly operating budget for the first year.

- Develop an expected return on investment, or ROI, and monthly cash flow for the first year.
- Provide projected income statements and balance sheets for two-year period.
- Discuss your break-even point.
- Explain your personal balance sheet and method of compensation.
- Discuss who will maintain your accounting records and how they will be kept.
- Provide "what if" statements that address alternative approaches to any problem that may develop.

Operations

- Explain how the business will be managed on a day-to-day basis.
- Discuss hiring and personnel procedures.
- Discuss insurance, lease, or rent agreements, and issues pertinent to your business.
- Account for the equipment necessary to produce your products or services.
- Account for production and delivery of products and services.

Conclusion

➤ Summarize your business goals and objectives and express your commitment to the success of your business.

Once you have completed your business plan, review it with a friend or business associate. When you feel comfortable with the content and structure, make an appointment to review and discuss it with your banker. The business plan is a flexible document that should change as your business grows.

Owning a business is the dream of many people. Starting your business converts your dream into reality. There is a gap between your dream and reality that can only be filed with careful planning. As a business your dream and reality that can only be filed with careful planning. As a business owner, you will need to plan. The plan is to enable you to avoid pitfalls, reach your goals and to build a business that is profitable. If it is not profitable, how long will it be the fulfillment of your dream?

Preparing a business plan is the one most crucial step in starting a business. The business plan will be your guide to managing your business to success. It should contain all the pertinent information about your business. It must be beautifully written, factual, and organized. It must not contain statements that cannot be supported factually. Owning and operating a business is a continuous learning process. Research your idea and do as much as you can on your own, but do not hesitate to seek assistance from people who can provide the information you need to know.

Example: SMALL BUSINESS PLAN

1. **Business Description**
   a. Business Name
   b. Location
   c. Product/Service
   d. Mission Statement

2. **Market Analysis**
   a. Size of market served
   b. Advantages and disadvantages of product/service
   c. Who is my customer?
   d. Who is my competition?

3. **Marketing Plan**
   a. How will product/service be priced?
   b. What makes product/service different from other businesses?
   c. How will product/service be advertised and promoted?
   d. How will product/service be distributed?

4. **Management Plan**

    a. How will the business be organized?

    b. How many people will be employed?

    c. Do key people have expertise in product/service?

5. **Financial Plan (Monthly for three years)**

    a. Business expenses

    b. Sales revenue

    c. Break Even Point – When will sales match expenses

Every test in our life makes us bitter or better, every problem comes to break us or make us. The choice is ours whether we become VICTIM or VICTOR.

Pursuit a Life of Peace, Purpose and Prosperity is
yours just WRITE the VISION!
Habakkuk 2:2 And the LORD answered me, and
said, Write the vision, and make it plain upon
tables, that he may run that readeth it.

*Take Chances,
Take a lot of them. Because
honestly, no matter where you
end up and with
whom, it always ends up just the
way it should be. Your mistakes
make you who you are. You learn
and grow with each choice
you make. Everything is worth it.
Say how you feel, always. Be
you and be okay with it.*

Made in the USA
Monee, IL
10 February 2022

dc20b156-f2eb-4663-a97f-ddd1436dd20fR01